SPEAKING UNIVERSAL

"You Know What I Mean"

VICTORIA FABLING

BALBOA.
PRESS
A DIVISION OF HAY HOUSE

Balboa Press books may be ordered through booksellers or by contacting:

Balboa Press
A Division of Hay House
1663 Liberty Drive
Bloomington, IN 47403
www.balboapress.com
1 (877) 407-4847

Because of the dynamic nature of the Internet, any web addresses or links contained in this book may have changed since publication and may no longer be valid. The views expressed in this work are solely those of the author and do not necessarily reflect the views of the publisher, and the publisher hereby disclaims any responsibility for them.

The author of this book does not dispense medical advice or prescribe the use of any technique as a form of treatment for physical, emotional, or medical problems without the advice of a physician, either directly or indirectly. The intent of the author is only to offer information of a general nature to help you in your quest for emotional and spiritual well-being. In the event you use any of the information in this book for yourself, which is your constitutional right, the author and the publisher assume no responsibility for your actions.

Any people depicted in stock imagery provided by Thinkstock are models, and such images are being used for illustrative purposes only.
Certain stock imagery © Thinkstock.

Print information available on the last page.

ISBN: 978-1-5043-5116-4 (sc)
ISBN: 978-1-5043-5117-1 (e)

Balboa Press rev. date: 06/07/2016

ACKNOWLEDGEMENTS

Thank you very much Julie St John for the fun illustrations accompanying Chapters 2 and 9, and her parents John and Mary St John for their support on many levels. Because writing is an isolating, sedentary activity, I'd like to publicly thank my friend Cora Schiller for intuitively calling me just as I finished each chapter, so that we could hula hoop together.

PREFACE

Speaking Universal is a practical language which doesn't have to include speech and *does* include every living thing on Earth.

I was born in 1958, still remembering where I came from, and some months later, while in the backseat of my parents' car, got to re-experience Paradise kinaesthetically and visually. I was being shown that Love is a tangible feeling that hangs in the air, and changes Life. Nature became my best friend at an early age because I recognised that same frequency of Love interacting with me when I was outside playing.

I wrote this particular book for conscious, curious individuals like me who love our planet Earth. The techniques I share are more like 'practical play' and, by practising the techniques daily, we'll get even better results than a peaceful revolution.

If you have ever wondered what an alien may think of the strange species that hold devices to their ears for communicating even though the message is not important, then we are on the same page. I coined the phrase 'beam what you mean' because we can, and every living thing has beaming receivers.

We can also 'reveal what is unseen,' and save ourselves pain. Animals, birds, fish, insects, rocks, trees, plants (which I call 'nature,') easily interact and understand each other, know when to come out of hibernation, when to flee to higher ground, where to find their offspring or mate, and how to warn others of a pending earthquake or monsoon.

By Speaking Universal we become about as smart as nature which isn't separate from God; it is a loving, creative intelligence, on call 24/7.

I give you a brief synopsis, in my Introduction, of how I discovered and *dealt with* a gift which has asked to be shared with you. Each of the 33 chapters describes a different facet of this once common-place art of communicating with 'All that Is,' an art which, when mastered, will add a heightened awareness to your life.

This is my promise to you.

INTRODUCTION

What qualifies me, Victoria Theresa Fabling, to write a manual for Conscious Beings ready to usher in *this* Age of Enlightenment?

I remember some of my lessons from the Spiritual realm, and use these to explain the simple steps *you* can take in order to reconnect with Source. By taking these steps, you'll gain access to more of your potential which will serve you. I am also used as a channel for writing. I receive my information from a wise, kind place which is like having a night-light on so you don't have to fumble in the dark as you find the way to the bathroom at 2 am.

We are all born with gifts. Some of mine are 'out of this world,' yet are applicable to Mother Earth. I teach a Universal language and speak in metaphors. This doesn't make me more special than those with other skill sets. I am offering my gifts as *an addition* to your own because I see struggling humans, so overwhelmed with the physical that they cannot allow themselves to notice that the whole planet is in trouble. I see humankind hardly interacting with each other, not being empathetic, yet still hoping they'll be lucky in love and finances. My solution is to offer a more active approach, one in which *you get in the driver's seat* of your own car, and allow yourself to be taught 'advanced driving tips' so that you fairly fly in your vehicle, and time your trips so the lights are mostly green.

As a young pre-school child, I toured England and Scotland with my parents and was often asked by their friends to check where the resident ghost spent most time, and what she or he was wearing. These friends' homes were open to the public, so having a ghost was a 'draw.' Although I enjoyed ghost-spotting, I sensed the loneliness of each person trapped between worlds, so I asked to learn how to encourage people to be sensitive to their environments, to be empathetic and unafraid of the Spiritual realm. Speaking Universal demonstrates the many benefits of increased empathy.

My next game involved changing my energy to match that of my surroundings. Specifically, I played with five stones which, to me, became mice and moved towards me as if I were their mother mouse calling them. I played this game daily, from breakfast through to lunch time. The scientific name for this activity is telekinesis, and it comes in extremely handy if you have a mind to manifest things, such as a mate or money.

I started school, was delighted to learn how to write, and could hardly wait to do joined-up letters. As soon as I could do that, neatly, I set to work writing my first book, "Woodland Friends." My father was supportive by giving me note books, a cartridge pen and, of course, my last name, Fabling.

I really took to writing as a past-time which could influence people to see the beautiful and magical solutions to any and all problems. My style has remained a little child-like to balance the "thoughts that do often lie too deep for tears." (See upcoming page - Wordsworth's Ode: Intimations of Immortality)

I used to win money prizes for writing, content and neatness at the local flower shows, and then I had a new English teacher, Mrs Williams, who gave me a B– for the first essay I turned in to her at Ryedale School. I was so upset I stayed behind to challenge her. She said she'd marked me that way because I could do better. I then paid attention to what she wrote in red pen because she was teaching me good grammar, the importance of avoiding fragmentation and of using fewer descriptive words so as not to lose a reader. I left that school at sixteen with the Wrightson Trophy for Academic Excellence. I was proud even though my family said nothing.

Chapters 1 and 5 outline the basic steps for Speaking Universal.

My career path is varied, having started off in the fashion industry I became aware that my soul wanted more, so I co-founded The British Academy of Graphology and went on to become Britain's busiest graphologist. In 1991 I also started studying Spiritual Healing with the NFSH, The Healing Trust.

I now help you, Conscious Beings, to reach your full potential.

Each chapter is a taster, to stimulate your interest in taking the subject deeper as you reflect and then replace my examples with your own.

Indeed, I very much look forward to hearing about your adventures via the interactive form on my main website, **www.myspiritualmentor.com**.

Excerpts from **Ode: Intimations of Immortality from Recollections of Early Childhood** by **William Wordsworth**

Our birth is but a sleep and a forgetting: 60
The Soul that rises with us, our life's Star,
Hath had elsewhere its setting
And cometh from afar:
Not in entire forgetfulness,
And not in utter nakedness,
But trailing clouds of glory to we come
From God, who is our home:
Heaven lies about us in our infancy!
Shades of the prison-house begin to close
Upon the growing Boy

Hence in a season of calm weather   166
Though inland far we be,
Our souls have sight of that immortal sea
Which brought us hither,
Can in a moment travel thither

We will grieve not, rather find   184
Strength in what remains behind:
In the primal sympathy
Which having been must ever be

My Heart Leaps up when I Behold
by **William Wordsworth**

My heart leaps up when I behold
A rainbow in the sky:
So was it when my life began;
So it is now I am a man;
So be it when I shall grow old,
Or let me die!
The Child is the father of the Man;
And I could wish my days to be
Bound each to each by natural piety.

TABLE OF CONTENTS

TABLE OF CONTENTS

Chapter 1

SELF-KNOWLEDGE

"To thine own self be true" is a quote from Shakespeare which keeps me on track. Knowing who we are requires digging for clues. Our strengths are often the activities which bring most joy and satisfaction. We also have our unique way of perceiving the world around us. Each living thing tends to interpret what's outside itself through its own lens. We need to remember this because it's when we forget that misunderstandings take place.

Our dreams do a marvellous job of providing us with hidden storylines and symbols from our psyche, so keeping a dream journal is a great idea. I analyse handwriting for people who would like more self-knowledge, to find out what is still unconscious. Stuffing down unprocessed emotions and parroting parental habits is counter-productive to living authentically.

It seems to me that we have a choice as to whether to muddle through life, blending in with the crowd and getting sick so that we die of an illness, or deciding to be masters of our own fate. Genetics is simply a term used by the medical profession. You can totally decide to bypass your blood-line and be as adventurous and invincible as you dare.

Speaking Universal is as easy as **ABC**. It's a process which involves:

Asking, **B**eing patient (until you get an answer), and then **C**ommunicating.

This is the foundation and, in each chapter, I'll share more building blocks.

A sculptor, who attunes with a rock, communicating prior to chipping away, will very often reveal a masterpiece. We are sculptors of our own rock and, as we chip away and reveal ourselves, it is natural to feel exposed. We fear being judged because we have experienced how uncomfortable that feels. "If you don't want to be judged, don't judge" is something my sister told me and I like this because of its stunning simplicity. Judging is a habit we all need to discard and just doing that one thing facilitates freedom to be all you choose to be.

We become free to accept and be fully present with ourselves when we no longer expect acknowledgement, accolades or approval. The riddle hidden in the rock is that *we receive after we've achieved*.

Chapter 2

SURVIVING TO THRIVING

Empowered people, masters (from the word mastery,) don't need looking after. They couldn't really care less if they are entitled to free medical or a bus pass because they have learned enough about their body to recognise when they are out of balance and do something constructive to rebalance.

Masters are often about as smart as nature! They don't see themselves as superior to the birds who migrate, to the wild animals who flee from an area which is going to be flooded or left devastated by an earthquake. Masters Speak Universal hour by hour. They tune in to their intuition instead of turning on the TV to watch the weather forecast or news. They listen to an internal prompt which could be in the form of a dream or a nudge to leave the house at a certain time and, by so doing, cross paths with a friend who acted similarly. So, please build in freedom to follow hunches because, if your schedule is too rigid, you'll miss out on some serendipity.

We all have a sixth, seventh and maybe more senses, and the positive outcome of being empowered and disregarding mind control is that we get to use all of these regularly. Our multiple senses then become accustomed to subtle communication which adds to our quality of life and may also make a difference between life and death.

When humans were less sophisticated they would hear telepathic messages such as, "so and so is dying and wants to see you" or "I'm about to have our baby, come home with food soon." They would smell or sense danger and be aware that their body could be healed by eating a plant growing within six feet of their home. If a predator was about to attack, they'd sense that too – and they would kill game in order to eat just like other living things. Creatures and plants Speak Universal with each other. Birds, dolphins, whales, frogs and many other species spread joy by singing. Animals and birds sometimes raise the offspring of another species; they befriend each other and heed calls for help.

When wild and tame creatures need our cooperation, they 'send' telepathically for a human to notice them, and then help them out. Dogs are particularly good 'senders.' One night my mother heard a loud snuffling sound outside our back door. She called my sister and me and then we followed the hedgehog across our yard to the stable where his 'wife' was doing her best to feed four babies. Mrs Hedgehog was tired and hungry so, by Speaking Universal, the hedgehogs conveyed, "Please bring us a saucer of bread and milk," which Mrs Hedgehog lapped up noisily, while we got to watch the cute babies feeding from their mum.

Shortly afterwards, in the day-time, we heard a similar snuffling noise at the same door. There stood our tortoise, asking for his eyes to be bathed as he'd just ploughed his way up through the grass heap where he had been asleep for the winter months. We just knew this was his primary request, and to be offered a slice of cucumber was an added bonus. Cucumber was a new food for him, so he hesitated at first, but now it is a favourite, especially when he wakes up.

How many times have our eyes been drawn, almost involuntarily, to a plant which was calling for water or to be dug up and placed in a different spot? When we notice the beauty of a flower, we are communicating in a language of gratitude. We both feel energised by the exchange.

Humans have become accustomed to speaking words, and yet there is a sub-language which comes from our vibes and body language. We can communicate to a foreigner, who's pointing a gun at us, that we are not afraid. If we show respect and stay out of fear, we are less likely to be bullied. Just as we feel vibes, so do others, even if they don't admit it.

You can tell if someone is being genuine by testing to see if they are empathetic; do they pay attention, listen, show consideration and get on your wave-length? Empathy is an important skill for successful relationships and that naturally increases when Speaking Universal becomes an unconscious habit.

Chapter 3

RELATIONSHIPS

Relationships take on a myriad of forms, and yet have one thing in common – a successful one depends on authentic communication.

There are guidelines about how to behave in certain cultures and social situations which can be helpful. Our senses, especially common sense, give us the same information. By taking the time to tune-in or empathise with another person prior to picking up the phone or asking for a favour, we get feedback. What we do with this feedback is up to us, but we would be wise to be considerate of the other person, for if we are, they are more likely to talk to us.

If we are being extra sensitive to the needs of a baby and are not normally heart-centred, we are still being authentic. Our personality is just a hat, and when Speaking Universal we take off all our hats before we go through the ABC procedure of asking, being patient and then communicating. We begin to make life-changes based on more substance. Our reasoning includes intuitive hits as well as what may be kind, true and helpful. As a result we start to like ourselves more, and become increasingly motivated to take ourselves, our dreams and talents more seriously.

Sales people create a huge number of relationships and they wield a lot of power. They know how to persuade, convince and get paid. A great sales person would also be heart-centred and empathetic – able to sense that although this person probably doesn't need any more products, they would appreciate a call. A truly great sales person would simply relay information, including alternatives, and then let us make a decision to buy. Speaking Universal is a transparent way of communicating; those who use it will attract those who are trusting, so to take advantage of them would be scamming which could result in some kind of 'karma.'

Just a reminder, here, that although relationships involve talking, they are more about feelings, thoughts and actions. We are affected by thunderstorms, and our equipment is similarly affected by our mood swings, particularly frustration. When we get bent out of shape, that's also when things like our computers are more likely to overheat or malfunction.

The forest, the weather, a trip we are about the take, the moon, our beloved – we can Speak Universal to them all, for their Spirit hears and understands. If you ask the sun to shine for a few minutes on a special occasion, you'll find it usually does. Timmy tortoise regularly climbs out from his new hibernation spot, under the London Pride, on my birthday. The sending of prayers and good wishes brings about a feeling of peacefulness, causing the recipient to feel more at home in their own skin.

Chapter 4

COMMUNING

We each have the ability to dial into a frequency which another person or object is emitting. We may not choose to do this, but we can, and this enables us commune, and then switch channels back again. Communing means opening up and letting go of boundaries; and in so doing we allow information to flow through us. Mediums and healers are familiar with the art of communing, and it is a very loving art because people feel understood. I expect I'm not the only one to have yearned for adults to 'get' me and it is a huge relief when they do, like landing on a soft bed.

I was married, briefly, and I found marriage confining because, after the ceremony, we were considered a unit. Society currently promotes marriage, with the promise that being united is a worthy goal, and being one (a unit) takes us to a higher plane of loving. However, I was already in that plane when communing with nature and my best friends. So, for me, at thirty-three, marriage was a constriction as my husband was often away and, yet, we were expected to socialise as a couple. To be clear, I'm not anti-marriage. I just felt let-down by societal collusion.

Do you relate?

Love is an expansive energy which, I feel, objects to being confined to a set of social rules, including 'obey,' and that could be why people are getting disillusioned with the game of playing house, cut off from others. No one person can totally 'get' another all the time and we lose ourselves sometimes, so by having more freedom to socialise and explore we get to experience the excitement of Speaking Universal with a stranger. This stranger could take the form of a heart-shaped rock that seems to say, "Take me home and give this to your mate." When you do, and your loved-one appreciates the gift, you may well experience a tangible feeling of expansion.

Sometimes it is healthy to be apart – because we are a part of all that is anyway, and we begin to recognise that our uniqueness is special. We also grow in appreciation for the part we each play in the whole movie of Life.

Communing *and* being in relationship come together in meditation, which is a healthy practise for getting to know our core values as well as our limitless, multi-faceted selves.

Chapter 5

LEARNING

Learning involves openness to new ideas combined with a healthy sense of discernment so that we don't fill our plates with academic junk food.

One of the best ways to learn is through exploration and experimentation because the practical application then becomes clear. James Redfield was a great teacher for me because I tried what he wrote in "The Celestine Prophecy," taking steps into the unknown and choosing the path that was brightest. I travelled alone, with consciousness as my guide, in Greece and the American mid-west. I followed clues, and embarked on vision quests in physicality. I could've done dry tests, like paper day-trading on the stock market, but I didn't – I went on real journeys, even moved to Canada from Great Britain. What I discovered was that my intuition and willingness to have faith were better guides than logic and reasoning because they stretched my awareness, and took me completely out of my comfort zone.

Prior to this, at seventeen, when my real world was full of apparent lacks, I was introduced to Shakespeare and Wordsworth and could then relax because I'd found friends in the Spirit world who 'got me,' spoke my language. I had been writing poetry for years, incorporating the old English spellings in order to make a bigger rhyming vocabulary.

I already knew "The child is the father of the man" and to discover that William Wordsworth had used these lines over two hundred years previously, in "My Heart Leaps up when I Behold," was hugely validating. I also fell in love with his "Ode: Intimations of Immortality," so I included excerpts at the beginning of this book, because Wordsworth was/is Speaking Universal.

In The Ringing Cedars series, I read how Anastasia learned things without leaving Russia's taiga. She wanted to know the essence of Paris, so she travelled there in her consciousness. Even though this is a work of fiction, Vladimir Megré describes Anastasia's use of wonder. When we wonder, we imagine and extend our consciousness which results in very real learning, because we become limitless beings able to channel answers. To contrast this, take an encyclopaedia which is a research-based, factual sort of a book and you'll find many discoveries have now been deemed nonsense. Science is great, yet it is limited. Even Google gets updated.

Learning is an ongoing process. It is healthy for us to leave our comfort zones for a small period of time each day, and experiment with something new, even difficult. We may fall down or even fail, but by exercising our muscles in such a way that we become unafraid of fear, we score a huge victory. If you already do this, congratulate yourself because you will be inspiring others to do likewise. Well done!

If we are going to learn or say something it may as well be true, helpful or kind, and a way to test this is to use –

Another Speaking Universal Technique

With your hat (ego) off, centre yourself, feel part of all at is, and then ask 'All that is' (Universe) "Truth, it would be rewarding for me to study architecture?" If you feel light and an involuntary radiance takes hold of your body, perhaps even causes a smile, Truth agrees with you. Conversely, you could get a nothing response, or a pulling backwards plus heaviness – which communicates "no, this is not true for you; ask about a different choice of career."

Time plays a role in the appropriateness of learning and teaching. Mystics used to be tortured then killed, so that memory still lurks in the consciousness of many humans and animals who once alerted communities to imminent danger.

Every living thing under the sun needs to come together in harmony as it once did before we were civilised (a euphemism for 'cut off'.) Visionaries and mystics are now very much needed. We can volunteer our time to imagine, and then co-create, a peaceful, cooperative, inclusive and abundantly healthy planet Earth. We have wielded the power to create (and destroy) for years, and are now, collectively, honing our sensitivities so that what we are about to create is mutually beneficial. We are waking up to the mantra 'Planet before profit.'

We are not victims of time and space; rather, when we set an intention, that focus drives the necessary energy *to* us.

Chapter 6

BUSINESS

Business can be both heart-centred *and* profitable. Once upon a time, people took pride in learning a trade and then providing this within a community. Each community would have a tailor, grocer, baker, lawyer, doctor, builder, publican and a farmer. Each business owner provided something which was welcomed by the community, and they would each make a profit.

When Speaking Universal it is possible to sense when a community member needs a helping hand. If someone can't get to the shops then a shopkeeper can make deliveries and, by so doing, gain repeat custom.

Running a business is a privilege. People put trust in the business owner and, while expecting to pay for quality and good service, they also assume that what they buy has been made with love and will live up to its claims.

When business is conducted the old-fashioned way people feel heard, they are proud to wear their new suit or recommend the latest café. Restaurant owners, who care about their customers, cook with love, and buy the best ingredients. We can taste the difference and our body recognises that it's been given good nutrition, so we gladly recommend their restaurants. The traditional model works, and buying local produce is a smart thing to do, because when individuals shop local, the whole community gets to know each other, networks and prospers.

When businesses ignore the principles of Speaking Universal, 'the getting of customers' becomes either a study in marketing or an avoidance of scams. Morality becomes a moot point.

Sales people are trained to elicit an emotional response from us, so it is wise to remember this. As customers, we can reverse this trend by Speaking Universal with ourselves prior to making life-changing purchases. "Truth, this product lives up to its claims?" If it does, you'll get a "yes;" and if not, you'll feel 'the weight of doubt,' even a full-bodied "no."

It's when a combination of our senses tell us that something is a good, solid proposition, likely to add value to our lives, we'd be 'sens-ible' to proceed.

Chapter 7

HEALTH

Being healthy is a team effort in which our spiritual, psychic, mental, emotional and physical bodies get to interact with each other in unique ways for the benefit of all. Having our own identify as well as five team members to consult is authentically empowering.

When we try to be anything other than authentic we get sick, and sickness is like receiving a message from the Source of Truth. Imagine playing a game whose aim is to share the ball between our five bodies so that they all feel they are winning. If we ignore the spiritual, the psychic and the emotional, paying attention only to our mental and physical selves, then our intuition about what we need to navigate eventually gives up saying, "over here!" We can stuff down the psychological pain but it eventually rears its head and stops play.

There are clichés out there which clamour to be heard and believed, such as, "it's genetic." I managed to dodge the blood-line, and the medical system, preferring to listen to what my five team players said, and if I can do so for the overall benefit of the real me, then I suggest – so can you. Trying to fit in with my tribe, my family of origin, caused me great distress because I was training myself to switch off my lights in order to be loved by them, and it didn't work anyway because I was rejecting myself. No blame – as I now understand that *my focus* was 'rejection.'

My skin is an accurate barometer; it fires up in the presence of negativity and if I get irritated or angry at the ridiculousness of my taking on other people's hurt, I increase the inflammation. There is no win/win here, so I make alternative choices such as forgiving someone, not returning to a house haunted by anxiety or backing off from someone who enjoys complaining.

Pets, trees, fossils, guides and crystals offer to take on some of our pain so that we don't have to suffer as much. They become surrogates, giving unconditional love as a way of Speaking Universal. I used to tell my budgie of my sadness while he cuddled up to me, crooning and regurgitating his birdseed. He was probably also absorbing my hurts into his body and, despite developing a tumour, he stayed alive until the afternoon I'd taken my final high school exams. I loved him very much, and trust he knows.

Chapter 8

MANIFESTING

Would you like to experience yourself as an empowered co-creator? We are already co-creators, just not always consciously manifesting, and when our lives are not going the way we want, we are in lack and we add to lack.

Mathematics isn't my strong point, but I did find it interesting that a minus number added to a minus number equals even less! This was a truth that I converted into my life as a young adult. I made an agreement with my ego and team players (spiritual, psychic, emotional, mental and physical bodies) that I would not judge anything even if it was 'normal' behaviour in society all around me to complain about or send a barbed thought to their employers. Instead, I stayed grateful that my bosses were paying me, and giving me a chance to gain work and life experience.

What I knew, instinctively, is that if we are given bad news, we can make it twice as bad if we add an opinion or silent swear word. The other person can feel a telepathic barb and so, in effect, you end up having a sparring match over an imaginary tennis net, and gain zero points. Sharing our woes is a habit, I get that, but I am sharing some advice which works. If you can stay in neutral and not allow any fear energy to form, you will usher in good fortune. Without drama, one door will close, yes, and because you'll have no added energetic baggage, you'll have an awareness to notice another door opening plus a willingness to enter a new realm of possibilities.

There is a grace period of time, a quarter of a minute in which we can slip up and have the inkling of an unhelpful thought, and then 'un-do' it by changing our focus onto something simple like, "I wonder which elevator light will shine red next?" I also bless the situation or notice something beautiful, like the colour of lipstick being flattering. That's what I did when my first boss fired me. The conclusion was – she changed her mind, and asked another department in Simpsons of Piccadilly to employ me for the rest of the month. I'd manifested a helpful outcome to what didn't look promising as the elevator was going down five floors from the fashion buying office to the basement.

What helps most with manifestation?

Using the fifteen seconds to focus on a blessing or beauty; maintaining a sense of joyful wonder and then communing with what you are calling in.

19

Realising that you are like a door way, and what you are manifesting comes knocking at your door sort of saying "You called?"

Be aware that some people are drains and others are radiators, and do your best to step aside the drains.

Invent your personal way of preparing for the day and commit to this on waking and before sleep; this will increase your inner strength.

Chapter 9

THE ART OF LIVING

Hidden within this title is a clue, take away the first T and, if we are willing to live open-heartedly with the risk of being *broken*-hearted from time to time, then we can live extraordinary lives of passion and fulfilment. We can say at the end —"I gave my All, and my All seemed to reward me in ways I couldn't conceive 'til I took action."

By eliminating the "be," and the "ve" from "believe," *lie* hides in plain view. Despite being raised to skim along the surface and *believe* the truths from bibles, elders and betters, I tended to question things, noticing discomfort when my five team-mates were not on-board with collective thought.

There was an historical event when I was eleven. The whole school was made to watch it on TV. I then went home to my mother, who was ironing sheets in the kitchen, and asked her if I could go to a special school because I was upset we'd been fed propaganda 'as if' news. Special schools, like Waldorf, hadn't reached Yorkshire, England, where we lived, so all I really had the power to do was be grateful we didn't yet have a TV at home, and that I could still write and study without the ever-present, invasive chatter-box which took pride of place in the homes of my friends and neighbours.

Questioning, reflecting and testing truth is sound advice, and you will already know this because of what tends to happen when we forget. Presidents are elected on one word promises which we so much would like to believe. Do you remember "Change!?" On reflection, which is difficult to do with 'group think' all around us, not all change is beneficial, and it is possible to launch ourselves "out of the frying pan, into the fire."

Remember to test Truth often, as mentioned in Chapter 5's Another Speaking Universal Technique.

In summary, get your ego to go and play elsewhere, and then **A**sk, **B**reathe (wait), and be ready for the **C**ommunication of a "yes" or a "no."

"Yes" is a palpable lightness of being, accompanied by an involuntary smile and/or forward motion. "No" is a heavy nothingness, accompanied sometimes by a backwards rocking of your body when in a standing position.

I encourage you and, as I write, remind myself, to constantly question, test and reflect. Becoming a mystic in your own right and then following your star is so worthwhile, because you can ask about career choices, potential lovers and where to set up home. I guarantee you'll receive customised feedback this way, which is more reliable than listening to a friend's advice.

Chapter 10

POWER OF WORDS

An aunt used to say "poor Victoria," and was, I felt, unconsciously adding to my woes by casting a spell on me that I'd have a lack of money.

"Abracadabra" followed by whatever you want to create is a spell, and so is "poor." Doctors unwittingly cast spells by giving a timeline to how long you've got left, so do mechanics when they diagnose a car.

If someone simply shrugs off a statement as being of little or no consequence, it probably will not affect them; the words will have no power. I resisted the label of poor and, as you know, what we resist tends to persist, so it seemed to lurch towards me as if I had to obey. I share this tidbit because, although we are subjected to a barrage of opinions, we become less vulnerable once we know we have the power to ignore them.

From a young age I started keeping a list of helpful words to use instead of those which compromised the truth, and I share some with you here. Please feel free to use any or all and then add some.

Helpful words	Unhelpful ones
Give it a go	Try (no skin in the game)
Fantastic!	To die for!
Bring it on	I'd kill for that
All the best	Break a leg
How are things? ((general)	How are you? (health focus)
I would like	I want, I don't have
I'm sorry to hear that	Poor
I can think of nicer things	I hate my job
I actualise, claim or need	I deserve
You're welcome	Good job! (the child is
Thank you	eating, not working!)
I love you	Depreciative name tags
Is this a good time?	Hey guys (I'm female)
I can, I choose, I will	I can't, should, ought
And	But

Chapter 11

ENTRAINMENT

We can learn in a plant-like way, via a combination of symbiosis and osmosis. When we agree to do this, we are agreeing to be up-graded simply by being in the presence of a greater source of wisdom and joy.

Some people travel to India and China to sit with a monk, and to receive energetic downloads in addition to Keeping Right Company, which I will explore with you in Chapter 16.

I am more of a leader than a follower, so I am not called to do such a thing, but I do deliberately go out in nature and ask permission to learn from the elemental kingdom. I enjoy spontaneous, synchronistic happenings and so that is what I choose to down-load. I make a fairy garden wherever I live, and tread lightly upon the planet because I realise all things are connected.

Entrainment is very easy to experience because it usually just involves an awareness that you are in wiser company and an acceptance of subtle changes which happen automatically. These changes affect each of us in different ways. For example, I was once applying some window film in the home of a couple; a week later I got a 'thank you' email from the husband letting me know that his wife was now pain-free. I'd tinted glass panes, consciously, with the result that my customer's physical pain left her. By doing your craft consciously you will affect people in a similar way.

I now play on the double-entendre of pain because I don't think the Universe is hot on spelling or deciphering which of several meanings. "Long to reign over us" is also open to interpretation.

Seriously, though, we can hold a crystal, a fossil or a piece of ammolite and realise we are being changed, in real time. By holding such things we are giving permission to accept their frequency and stored information which we can use. This is another example of entrainment whereby we are the student, and a sentient living thing is only too willing to impart knowledge.

Mike McDonald shared a tree story with me. When one of his daughters went missing he leant on a tree in Qualicum Beach and asked where to look. He received a clear reply, "in Victoria," and that's where Mike found her. Inspired by this tale, I went to the forest and asked a tree for help designing my next business card, whereupon I was shown a globe.

Chapter 12

ABSOLUTELY!

Would it be a relief to you to know there are no absolutes anywhere in the Universe?

We make promises and vows to love and obey forever, and strive for perfection, hoping perhaps that this will make us more spiritual. What if we were to consider our uniqueness as one of our finest qualities, and to be able to co-exist harmoniously with other realities in which our understanding of physical matter is turned on its head? On Earth there are places where gravity goes into reverse; not so long ago telegrams were delivered by the postman whereas now people text on tiny devices; new colours and sequences appear in rainbows; there are autistic, disabled children who are active ambassadors for peace, and who communicate with message boards (as well as via telepathy.) I participated in a Psychic Children's conference organised by James Twyman during which adults were receiving lessons in the art of living from a group of children who couldn't speak or use their limbs 'properly.' If you'd like a transcript from this conference, let me know. The children channelled this information, and we could certainly feel the purity of their exchanges.

If you catch yourself saying things like "I'll always love you, I'll never forget you, it's impossible, incurable, unimaginable, inconceivable ...." you will have to eat humble pie because the idea that something *can't* be done automatically generates an example of it being done - an illogical but scientific truth of how life in the Universe operates.

If all life is designed to expand, then so are we and, by Speaking Universal, we can do so with less struggle and more awareness. This involves leaving our comfort zone, though, and agreeing to participate in Life's adventure.

There is one absolute. Universal consciousness exists in everything; that's why Mike McDonald asked a tree to locate his daughter. By acknowledging this, and approaching with awe, we open ourselves to a whole new level of communication, which is nurturing, inclusive *and* holistic.

Chapter 13

LABELS STICK

I'd far rather you totally immersed yourself in a good movie or novel, completely entranced by the story-line than 'believed' any label which has been given to you by a well-meaning medic, cleric or family member.

"She's shy," is a *horrible* label, and yes, I'm judging here. I heard that a lot when I was four years old, and I was fortunate that my mother would retort "My daughter is *not* shy!" on my behalf. Many children were not as fortunate and are now middle-aged men and women who say, "I don't go to dances or pubs because I'm shy," and then stay at home letting days and weeks and years go by. They could, of course, remove that particular egoic label from their mind by stating (with passion) – "Tonight I'm not listening to you, and I'm going out specifically to socialise," then actually follow through. The Universe would support them.

Challenging ourselves by doing something new or difficult each day develops a resourceful muscle so we can overcome all sorts of obstacles from shyness to arthritis. We needn't stay stuck to a label. When we become open to alternative perspectives, we also become more flexible in Life.

I facilitate healings for people, pets and places and, recently, when I asked to give spiritual healing to my neighbour to ease intense arthritic pain, she reminded me that she was due to get her third surgery, a shoulder replacement. I felt the expansion of her energy bubble, saw the sun start shining the moment I asked for its assistance, felt healing taking place and so did she, "I've got a buzz on ... it must be the medication," which didn't make sense, except as feedback to me that she was open to a lessening of pain, just not a miracle cure because she'd been told "arthritis is incurable."

Fortunately, pets and places do not have such scepticism. Bonnie the dog had a broken leg so she called me telepathically. When I arrived (unexpectedly for her owner, Catherine), she moved her leg towards me so I could direct energy healing. Bonnie was soon out of pain and my friend Catherine didn't have to pay another vet's bill. In Great Britain, a 'nation of animal lovers,' pets go to healers as a first option because their owners know healing works, is more convenient *and* saves them money!

Chapter 14

SOLUTIONS ARE NEARBY

Shamanic wisdom teaches that for every ailment there is an antidote in nature within walking distance, and failing that – a healer who can undo the fright and put in its place a psychological order which the body will then obey in order to get well instantly or after the fever breaks.

If you didn't grow up close to nature, the solutions are still planted nearby. There will be a remedy in your pantry or garden, and, if not, a neighbour will just happen to come round and say something wise, such as: "These are symptoms of drinking too much pop, so before you panic at the label of MS, how about taking out aspartame from your diet?" Neighbours and health store owners very often play the role of healer or sage, reminding us that the famous clinic which is far away and expensive is not our only option. Even though the word 'cure' is not permitted in advertising, the action of *being cured* is only limited by our own imagination; it happens a lot, daily, and is overlooked by the media because it is not in their remit. They are supposed to go along with the 'group-thought' of, "If you're sick, go to the doctor," (and support the pharmaceutical companies, who are in bed with the media, rather than your health.)

For every problem in life there is a creative solution, and we can all observe that this law is Universal. When there's a shortage of mothers in the wild we see animals being adopted, and loving their siblings. Humans, who have raised a male lion cub and then returned it to the wild, are not only recognised, but introduced to the fully grown lion's own pride years later.

There are also thousands of stories of prisoners who have escaped atrocities, of homeless people who make good, and of people who were cruel having to experience some of their own karma. One solution to not being able to afford a car is to accept it and ride a bike: there are of course several other solutions to this scenario.

Necessity seems to fuel creative growth, and when any living thing *has* to adapt, they give it a go, and then often prefer this new way of life because it feels more fully satisfying. Using our hearts is brave in a society used to strategising. I'd rather be brave than disconnected. How about you?

Chapter 15

HOME

"There's no place like home" seems to be universally true.

In nature, as well as in our society, everything needs a familiar nesting or resting place which provides protection, shelter, warmth, water and a view, (because we are all curious beings.) If a home lacks some of these elements, we move, even though moving is highly stressful and risky.

Zoos and animal farms are not necessarily cruel places provided the creatures are well cared for because the various species seem to enjoy their extended, exotic family. They have no predators and don't have to worry about walking or flying or swimming long distances before they find food and new lodgings. Instead, they can enjoy a life which has in-built variety and seems like a luxury hotel compared to a camp site. When bears and monkeys have found themselves 'free' they also had to make a choice to stay free or return of their own accord to their safe place with a door which protects them from the world.

My ideal home has many rooms because I 'play' many roles and feel most alive when I can write in one room, undisturbed, and then entertain in another where I can invite friends; sleep in another room, preferably with someone I love. I like leaving my home, too, because I enjoy Speaking Universal, and yet I come back, grateful for my nest so I can sleep in peace.

How is it for you? Do you yearn to go back home, if so – what qualities does home hold for you, and could you conjure up a way of having your cake and eating it? For me, so long as I have like-minded friends, high enough ceilings, quiet nights, sunshine and minimal radiation, I can adapt. If I were to find myself in a basement suite or a noisy street, I would leave.

When we don't have to waste energy looking for pastures new we can create deeper friendships and look at the world with wonderment. We become excited to be alive because we have that extra energy ... unless we forget to *Keep Right Company*, which is also essential; because we are influenced by the energies we let into our sacred space.

Chapter 16

KEEP RIGHT COMPANY

By now you will have noticed that with some people, and in some places, your whole being seems to expand and your heart feels full to overflowing. You feel good around these people and the feeling is mutual. That is *Right Company.*

When you are around another person and are feeling constricted, inarticulate, confused, tense and sick or drained, you are experiencing warning signals. Your energy is either being taken or blocked, so your best course of action is to make your excuses and leave. If the person is in your space, put on an imaginary blue cloak as a disguise, create a bigger energy bubble around yourself or simply tell *them* they need to go. This is not a time to be 'nice.' We all pick up entities from people who have played the victim role for too long, and then have to do extra laundry – theirs and ours!

It is vitally important to Keep Right Company and set sensible boundaries, for otherwise your connection with the Universal Source is lost or depleted, and you are at risk of being picked as easy prey by anyone who is hungry for energy. Bear in mind, playing the victim to get their needs met is far easier for them than going through a self-awareness process which accesses their own power and connection to Source.

People in the caring and service professions need to make an extra effort to keep their vibration high by focusing on the pleasant things in their surroundings, and making sure their social life is spiritually, mentally and emotionally restoring.

There are times when a one-way energy flow between people and animals is a healthy thing. Also, when young children set up friendships with their grandparents the collective energy is given or taken as and when needed.

Right Company includes nature, your guides, nutrition, inspiring literature and music. Find time to reflect, be peaceful, to move towards things which elevate your mood, including exercise. You have a duty to get to know and be happy with your own company. Paradoxically, when you *are* content alone, you are seldom left alone, for you have a secret to which others would like the answer.

Chapter 17

UBUNTU

If you are Keeping Right Company and are excited to expand your awareness to influence the whole world without tools or manipulating anyone then you'll probably feel at home with Ubuntu.

This movement was formed by Michael Tellinger in South Africa, and his website is **www.ubuntuparty.org.za**.

In a nutshell, you find and focus on a familiar object in the centre of your community, such as an old oak tree or red phone box (two things which have emotional significance for Brits.) You can then, collectively, send your vision/idea for 'greater understanding' or 'get well soon, we love you very much,' to this object which becomes a message board. People post, telepathically, on this board, and they also go there for inspiration or news.

Nomads send messages to the moon, and trust that their loved ones will look up, tune in, and receive the message at night time. I chose the moon too, standing alone in a remote country lane in North Yorkshire, England, because our house phone was for adults only. Necessity is a brilliant teacher, and I learned something which worked via tuning into what was already in place in African countries. African nomads also use the biggest tree as a message station; wives ask their husbands to return from a hunting trip or simply send their love along the airwaves, and the husbands scan the ether, find their familiar tree and send a message back. When a group of Africans was asked what they would most like to buy, they replied "a phone," not yet fully appreciating their own 'smart' skills.

I had used, without knowing, a shamanic practise when I was a teen reaching out for an affection-connection. My moon-generated practise created a portal to the heart of African culture, and brought to our house in Yorkshire for Christmas 1974, Asefa Seifu, and his girlfriend Mulu. They had fled Ethiopia because of the revolution and were a God-send to us because my father had died in September, and my mother, sister and I were still struggling to communicate with each other. With open-hearted company, our house felt like home again and we all toasted "absent friends."

In the summer of 1981, in Brighton, UK, the Fountain Method was born which you may like to look up on You Tube, via Facebook or www.tongo.org.uk. Everyone is welcome to use this method instead of or as well as the one I have outlined above. Tongo is currently suggesting we send a combination of Divine white light and earth energies to a focal point at 7 pm on the 27th of each month. You may also be interested in joining www.thesilentminute.org.uk and sending a focused prayer for peace at 9 pm every night wherever you are in the world.

Chapter 18

COUNTERINTUITIVE

We have experimented with intuition which becomes the lead ingredient in Speaking Universal, and yet sometimes doors remain firmly barricaded. At such times we can love, consider ourselves spiritual, do our clearing 'work', our self-awareness 'work' and still suffer so much that we have to turn to an expert for help.

If this resonates with you, perhaps you will take heart from a couple of my experiences from 1994 when I was married, and working at a nearby job which didn't delight me but provided income.

I lay in bed one Thursday night after my husband had come back from his weekly military briefing. He was asleep, processing highly classified stuff, and I was totally shocked to receive this through *my* brain. I didn't really appreciate learning how we can hypnotise in order to cause a car accident on cue.

I called out silently yet earnestly for help from the spiritual realm with all the strength I could muster, "What should I believe?" and it was Jesus who answered with gold letters written in the dark, followed by a booming male voice saying "The Truth is within you!" and to make sure I received the message, my tea cup fell off the side of the bath tub as the house vibrated.

I then started having panic attacks. I had received information which I wished I hadn't, countered by a visit from The Son of God, yet I was the one feeling like I'd been to war. I came back from work the following Thursday, immediately reached for the Yellow Pages directory; looked under psychics and phoned the only number. An older man answered and said he could help, free of charge, because he could see that I worked in an old school house which had not been bombed in the war. My panic attacks seemed to have been caused by trapped souls who'd returned to the only familiar place still standing and who also sensed I could set them free. I had simply not understood their messaging style! The man on the other end of the phone asked if I'd be patient and take each ghost to the light. I agreed, and an hour later, we'd freed well over a hundred.

So, interception of the army briefing and panic attacks had not been signs of weakness; I was in the process of becoming clairaudient, clairvoyant and clairsentient!

Chapter 19

IT'S NOT MINE!

When I was suffering from panic attacks and having trouble sleeping without intercepting my husband's thoughts, I could have gone to a doctor for a prescription and sick leave note. It was counterintuitive to pray when I was conflicted in my beliefs and it was out of the ordinary to dial a psychic, yet both actions resulted in empowering outcomes.

Family members tend to project their stuff onto each other and then attack those they really love. This behaviour is a counterintuitive cry for help.

I have lived and worked in London, England, using the crowded subway (tube) system for five days a week without feeling drained by the thousands of people travelling with me. I have also been a care-giver in a quiet town in Canada and felt zapped immediately on entering a client's home. Logically, you would expect a large city, teaming with all sorts of life forms, dealing with all sorts of issues, to cause tiredness. What actually happens is we *share* energies when we are constantly moving, talking to, and colliding with each other, and what rubs off can contribute more than deplete. If we don't know the people, we don't open up as much and thus don't give our implicit permission to be drained. At the end of the day we can review, be grateful for, clean off, and empty our proverbial cart of thought forms.

If we go into nature and live a more reclusive life-style the negativity *we* build up is neither challenged nor dissipated, so that's how we can feel worse in so-called Paradise than we ever felt in the thick of things. Lots of stuff we pick up is not ours, and some, which comes to light eventually, *is*, and can be discarded easily if we choose a life of joy, grace and ease. Struggling is usually the result of an unchallenged psychic program, handed down from a parent, and then hardwired into our brains.

Happily, there is a solution. We can stop running on automatic, pause, claim control and repeatedly make informed choices until we become powerful *creators* instead of passive *reactors* - (same letters, new sequence.) I used to take the most circuitous, difficult route, and now I am playing with each day, allowing its energy to work with mine.

Chapter 20

QUESTIONS ARE ANSWERED

In June of 2015 I was ready for Access Consciousness® because Janette, one of my friends, recommended the course material as an add-on to my tool kit of healing techniques. Access® is about staying in the question because there are unlimited solutions.

I bought myself a small spiral bound note book and started writing down open-ended questions, some which are used regularly by Gary Douglas and/or Dr Dain Heer, his business partner. I also created my own.

Janette had been stopped by a police officer for speeding, and she used this Access Consciousness® question, "What else is possible?" The officer was very polite and said Janette had an immaculate driving record which he didn't feel inclined to spoil. A few weeks later, when I was stopped for distracted driving, looking at the beautiful homes in Chemainus, I refused to feel fear and asked "How can life get any better?" *My* officer asked me if I was alright. He then let me go on my way once I promised him that, although I was tired, I would really focus as I drove back to Qualicum Beach.

My questions relate to the real life issues that come across my path. People phone me in distress hoping that I will have a magical solution or that I will listen. I find listening to such stories draining, so my mind goes to the magical solution option. This is where you ask questions, issue proclamations, declarations and generally distract the egoic mind which has caused the problem to escalate.

The art of asking clever questions involves a banishment of judgement, so our Creative Intelligence is able to ask for help, confident that a personal reply will be delivered. You'll recall from Chapter 18 that when I asked whoever was listening, "What should I believe?" I received an immediate response. From this, I learned that, when asking a question, it is courteous to wait for a reply. If I'd asked a hypothetical question, "Why is this happening to me?" I'd have been in victim-mode, venting rather than being open to a clear reply. I'll expand on 'Whys' aren't Wise in Chapter 28.

Chapter 21

LOGIC AND PROGRAMS

When you choose to Speak Universal, you'll be setting aside logic and your analytical approach to life in favour of calling in a higher level of intelligence, which can then be *supported* by human reasoning/research.

Humans who don't care to see the interconnectedness of all things will use clever marketing strategies to benefit themselves. They are usually not motivated to be open-minded because 'switching horses' tends to be expensive, whereas a brand, once established, can make them a fortune in repeat business. They rely on research, obtained by others with a limited perspective, and then organise their lives around second-hand information which tends to get disproved forty years later. Fashion and architecture also have forty year cycles. Facts don't tend to remain facts because the creative intelligence opens doors to infinite possibilities. Common sense implies using all of our senses and *is* usually reliable.

We have a number of programs running inside ourselves, and we also have an 'off' switch. We have the keys to that switchboard, and here's a selection of assumed programs which could be challenged.

Programmed statements being challenged

It's genetic.	Not if you decide otherwise
Self work is necessary.	Really? I'd better tell the President
I'm getting old.	No wonder, then, that you look your age
Old age sucks.	You obviously keep 'wrong' company!
I need glasses.	How about doing eye exercises?
Blood is thicker than water.	Wasn't in my case
You must get a degree.	Could this be a banking scam?
I'm not good enough.	Excellent self-fulfilling prophecy!
It's impossible.	I won't even consider the idea

Scientists and researchers don't meet regular people performing extraordinary feats of endurance or spontaneous healings because they are not interested in losing their jobs. When someone is adamant that it's their way or the highway, you could either duck out of the conversation or say, inside yourself, "that's an interesting point of view" (IPOV – used in Access Consciousness®.) Programs just send. If you 'Speak Universal' you send, receive, delete and recreate for the good of planet Earth and beyond.

Chapter 22

SMOKE AND MIRRORS

Telling the truth, being authentic and transparent is a high ideal, one to which I aspire and yet there is a time and a place for magic while still Speaking Universal.

I was inspired by the dandelions on my lawn which had long gangly bodies covered by a skinny camouflage suit the colour of burned grass during the afternoon and early evening. These same dandelions, in the cooler times, looked like yellow chandeliers swinging upside down from a green electrical cord; this playful energy was attracting the bees to pollinate.

The dandelions provided a metaphor for smart behaviour. When we need to be invisible we can contain our energy and emit less of our personality. There are times to shine, such as during a talent show, and there are other times when shining is interpreted as provocation which, in turn, brings about discord and sometimes death.

I was saddened to learn that a prominent female healer challenged a group in a place she calls the 'Under-underworld.' What was she thinking? These beings, who didn't appreciate her superior attitude, attacked and rendered her comatose for five weeks. We are not the only living beings in the cosmos, and to assume a position of 'better than' is considered rude. When we stop judging, we become safer and freer.

Bullying is far less likely to happen if the bully doesn't smell any fear from us or sense that we may be a threat to their way of life. With practise we can break the tension in a room full of people by embodying a frequency which is higher, brighter and more entertaining. Joy is an obvious choice, especially when done with subtlety so that people assume that their mood just lightened of its own accord.

How do you do this? This is simply a decision and a follow-through exercise which you put into action and repeat until you achieve mastery.

Chapter 23

MANY PLAY LATE

Unconditional love is revered. People give unconditionally to their pets and their pets give them unconditional love in return. A tally isn't taken of who gives what during their open-hearted communication, so it *seems* the bond has nothing to do with ownership.

Nevertheless, anything which is having most of its needs met by another living being, is also 'playing' a game, and the provider does a considerable amount of extra 'work' such as getting up early to feed the horses, pruning, watering, feeding, fertilising, cleaning and maintenance. The provider tends to overlook 'the elephant in the room' which is the lack of leisure time to enjoy companionship, their swimming pool and nicely mowed lawn. They also forego spontaneity because they can't leave their dogs, horses or the garden for long.

Speaking Universal helps us to become aware that we are vulnerable to manipulation from our gardens, homes, family, pets, and friends. Once we are aware, we are free to love who, what and how we choose. Think back to a summer's day when you ran in a meadow and lay for hours in the long grass watching butterflies playing in a clear blue sky and recall how this seemed to energise you. If you then switch to a more recent memory of mowing the lawn, putting the sprinklers on, and then trimming the edges, you may start to feel exhausted at the very thought.

My point is we have options, such as enjoying a picnic at the beach instead of on the lawn, and having a vegetable rather than a flower garden at home.

We are manipulated by the media; yet *you* can decide against having cable, to talk with your family rather than hide behind a computer, newspaper or video game, that sort of thing. When I was a child, my family was scared of philosophical conversations so, although my attempts with *them* bombed, I'm sure some of you will succeed with openers to deeper conversations, such as, "What do you value most about living here?" as well as questioning before buying. You can ask things like, "How will I spend my weekends if I do buy acreage and a couple of horses for the kids?" or, "If I buy a boat, how many times a year will I use it?" and "Will this be rewarding?"

Chapter 24

EGO WE LOVE YOU

"I am an Entertaining Go-getting Organiser" said Ego Consciousness. "Living things would be bland without personality."

I agree, absolutely! When I say, "Take off your ego, like a hat, and reach into another realm of consciousness," your ego is still in the car with you, except your spiritual essence is the one driving while your intuition is map-reading or following the GPS.

Our egos like to be in control, and we are giving them the 'holiday experience' which is intended to be fun and renewing for the whole of us. We appreciate the years of hard slog our egos have put in to keep us safe and grounded, disciplining us to avoid unnecessary risks.

Comedians and actors are skilled at keeping their ego commentary in the back-seat so that they can empathise and even slide into the skin of another character. We feel moved by their ability to convey an embarrassing moment in a way that causes laughter, and thus frees us from our tendency to be self-critical. When we meet a truly great entertainer, we are also relating to an authentic individual who has made a loving agreement with his or her ego to check-in with all five team players who, in turn, feel the audience, second by second, adapting with ease.

Humans aren't the only species to have an ego. When our family tortoise was introduced to a mate, Timmy was not at all impressed and stopped her coming out of her shell. Timmy *liked* being the king of his domain. He rather liked 'playing' humans too, as he'd taught us how to groom him and what he liked to eat, when. He also invented a fun game. He'd wait 'til someone was on the sun-lounger, and then position himself underneath so that by standing on his toes, his shell pushed their body up a couple of inches. Watching mating dances is also a wonderful way of observing ego in action, isn't it?

When we lose our tendency to be self-conscious, we reach out to others without fear of rejection and, by so doing; we're able to contribute positively. That's an ideal time for an accolade like, "Ego, we love you."

Chapter 25

BE A LERT!

When talking about serious subjects, ones which can be provocative even when that is not my intent, I add a touch of humour.

I still use a bookmark saying, "Be a Lert! The World needs more Lerts." I'm sure you'll agree that it does and that in this instance the word 'need' is simply factual without the 'poor me' connotation.

By being alert, we rise above or slither away from manipulation because we have seen the signs before, and may have suffered heart-break coupled with a loss of a home. I've been there and didn't realise at the time of making a couple of major decisions that the Universe is usually encouraging when we are poised to do something creative. Even if the decision turns out to be life-changing in ways we didn't anticipate, the Universal Intelligence which we *did* consult, still remains unruffled, viewing it as a Growth Opportunity, "GO!" for short.

When dealing with worldly things, I now have a few tools which keep me streetwise. I'll share what I use, and find reliable.

First of all I get an intuitive feel, and then I excuse myself in order to ask, "Truth, will this course of action be rewarding," mentioned in earlier chapters. Speaking to Truth focuses the Universal Intelligence to a specific stream of knowledge; therefore, I am not leaving myself open to experiencing another random 'GO.'

Contracts with people are where I've found handwriting analysis invaluable because handwriting accurately conveys our intent. (I used to be Britain's busiest Graphologist.) It is unusual to ask someone for their signature prior to signing yours, but it can be done. B, d, o, p and q open at the base, hook-like j, y or g's and illegible or crossed out signatures are red-flags. A contract is designed to protect the *other* party, so taking it with you, refusing to be rushed, is a way of being street-smart. If you can't do this, then tape the person's replies to your questions, and then go to the washroom to play the recording via a reverse speech app. The truth will come out in slow, audible words. You can then make an informed, empowered decision.

I go into Graphology in greater detail in my website, **www.myspiritualmentor.com**.

Chapter 26

FASTER THAN THE SPEED OF LIGHT

Magic moments keep us excited about life. When we see life through the eyes of a child, even as an adult, we can create miracles. Wonder is the glue. Phrases such as, "I wonder if" or "What can I contribute?" are a great start, and to expect a wonderful outcome is far wiser than to entertain worry. You are not being a Pollyanna; rather you become more like Merlin.

If someone were to call me out of concern for my safety, I would turn that around and ask them to hold the vision that the outcome will be even more favourable than either of us can imagine right now.

When I am facilitating healing and/or talking to a master in another dimension, I send my request and receive a response 'faster than the speed of light.' I add these six words at the end of my request because I am serious in my intent. Having released the request, a charge then shoots through my body like a mild electrical jolt. I send and receive this way in order to avoid interferences of any kind, and also out of respect. Beings less dense than us would otherwise have to adjust their energy levels, to *dumb down*, in and around the static of all our mind control/opinions. In order to channel information, the medium or channel vibes up, and changes gears back to a lower, slower frequency at the end of each session.

When you require specific help from a supernatural source, an emergency isn't the time to be shy. You simply submit your request faster than the speed of light, and get ready to experience a mild jolt or shiver as your request leaves, and another when receiving the response. You will be Speaking Universal as an equal and, instead of pleading, will be more powerful and more present in your body. These jolts do not need to be uncomfortable, and if they are, explain that some fine-tuning is necessary.

The Universe says "yes" most of the time, as it sees us as love-filled beings, like Itself, so if you have ever had the notion that suffering is normal or you need to be more worthy before asking a favour, please cancel that, and be open to creating a new reality – one of co-creation with the masters, guides and elementals. Co-creation is limitless and takes place in all time-lines and life-times known and unknown, simultaneously.

Chapter 27

GIFTS

Giving and receiving are two sides of the same coin. The rim is like our perception of things, physical and esoteric.

If you were to ask a group of people to demonstrate by a show of hands whether it is better to give or to receive, I expect you'd see more raised hands favouring 'to give.' The gift in the question is that it challenges us to reflect more deeply, because someone has to receive in order for the giving to take place. There can be no giving without receiving. If we sing joyful songs we are giving, and in the singing of the songs we become even more joy-filled. Life as duality is a fiction, I think, and when we refuse to play in the fiction parlour, we cease to judge and put external conditions on how/what and when we'd like to receive something.

I gift myself the chance to pick a certain quality from a pot containing Tyler and Drake's original angel cards, along with words which I've written and inserted. In the morning, before leaving my bedroom, I pick a card indicating how I'll 'work' with the Universe today, then another for how to show up for others (give to) and a third which is the energy I will receive.

One morning, while writing this book, I picked 'Love' as my primary energy, 'Receive' as my paradoxical gift *to* others, and 'Communication' *from* others, including my guides. This combination became a bubble of inter-connected energy which I accepted as Truth, that day for me. And I did feel I was channelling. The following morning's energy featured a completely different combination. I find this practise grounding because I can then focus on being a conduit for the specific energy combo I pick. Occasionally, I pick 'Surrender' or 'Willingness' and I know, when I do, that this won't be the day to paddle upstream in an attempt to have things go my way. At night time, I marvel at each performance we've pulled off, without a rehearsal. And I'm reminded - *Energy is a dynamic, which acts like a guide.*

When we are selecting a gift and our eyes are drawn to an object or service that we know resonates with our friend, we are allowing ESP to guide the object into our energy field. We can rely on this guidance, and when we do; we find that what caught our eye, and we buy, makes the perfect present.

Chapter 28

'WHYS' AREN'T WISE

Figuring things out and asking "why?" comes from our ego's need to know and be right.

What if being right was a shaky foundation anyway? I have changed my point of view and had my eyes opened for me many times, and I am sure that is the case with you. "What was I thinking, feeling or eating moments before my skin started itching?" is a more helpful question to ask myself than, "Why am I itching?" which could result in wasting hours on the internet looking at a whole gamut of research not at all related to the uniqueness of me. It is not my business to know all the whys, as they open a Pandora's Box of endless information, hence: *'Whys' aren't Wise*.

"Why did he/she leave without saying a word?" is a futile thing to ask. Even if you stored up the question and asked it later, the person may not remember, and has now been put on the spot in an accusing way, which is certainly not Speaking Universal. "What do I feel about this?" may give you an insight, and it will also remind you not to take things personally. When this happened to me recently I just sent a text message, "I'm sorry if I gave the impression you had to leave." A reply came back, "No worries."

"Why did he/she have to die?" takes the first example to an even more futile level because it repeats, like a lament. It isn't even a real question; rather it is an attempt at blame, 'wanting,' implying lack, of a response from the great complaints' department in the sky. The answer would be complex and many-layered, and most probably incomprehensible to us.

A lighter example (which implies discontent,) "Why do we always go to the same place on holiday?" could be rephrased as a specific request, "Please may we go to the Lake District this year." The chances of going to the Lake District are now much higher than they would have been.

Truth changes; nothing is absolute. "How," "what" and "where" are lead-ins which show that you've already given the question some thought and are willing to take action to back up the answer. Instead of steering towards an opinion, these three lead-ins open us up to fresh possibilities.

Chapter 29

IT'S OK TO HISS

If you were out walking in a forest and came too close to a snake, it would slither away or hiss. Creatures respect boundaries and let us know when they require space. A family cat will often ignore all but one or two visitors to the home, and a horse will behave in a similar way.

There remains a dual standard about the inappropriateness of being a 'yes' person. We know not to love too much, yet still carry an expectation that other living beings will be amenable to us when we ask for that feedback. Now that we are aware of this, because we are when we consider this, we can accept that the behaviour of other living things is beyond our control, and we are also free to discern whether hugging everyone we meet at church or spending a Sunday helping a friend is really a kindness.

When you start Speaking Universal as a living meditation, you can expect to receive "yes" more often than "no," because your intuition will have already hinted that this may be a suitable path. However, sometimes you will get a strong "no" to a question such as, "Would this treed area welcome our new home?" If you were to ignore the "no" and went ahead with clear-cutting in preparation to build, the land itself would rebel.

The town council would deny you a building permit, and then there would be numerous complications, even illness. This is a typical scenario when the land uses a human system to stick up for its rights. There are sacred areas which we must respect so they can continue contributing in positive way.

Portals, sacred sites and ley-lines act like our veins and arteries; we cannot just puncture one and start pumping in toxins without complaint. They do, however, gladly carry our love and creativity right round the planet. For fifteen years I stood in a certain spot in West Kelowna where I sensed an open door below and above me and, as I stood there, decreed that anyone crossing this ley-line with an open heart would have pure love energy bless them a hundred-fold. I then left Kelowna and ceased that practise. When I revisited the trail a couple of years later, confused as to where to call home, a coyote turned his head to look at me from the spot which had become a portal. My understanding of that symbolism, because it is not *that* normal to see a coyote in daylight is, "You left the path *and* it is still here for you."

Chapter 30

TRIUMPH AND DISASTER

"If you can meet with Triumph and Disaster and treat those two impostors just the same" wrote Rudyard Kipling in his famous poem, "If."

Speaking Universal isn't a quest for happiness, although we are happier when we are willing to be awake, aware of the interconnectedness of all things.

To be truly happy we will be grounded in knowingness that 'shit' happens, and when it does, we can take another breath and make a different decision without feeling 'hard done by.'

We can sense when and where to be exuberant, and when to show deep disappointment. A funeral isn't the best place for slap-stick humour, just as announcing plans to divorce at a wedding would be deemed 'odd.' We are masters of our emotional responses and have the innate fortitude to be content in less than idyllic circumstances. If we crow about or rail against our circumstances, our intensity repels and creates alienation, which is the last thing we 'want' to happen.

Timing plays a role in Speaking Universal. We sometimes push down an emotional response when we are working or in shock. This is completely understandable, yet we must still make time to acknowledge our hurts prior to letting them go. Spending time in nature at such times, the extremely happy and sad ones, will tend to serve you better than reaching for a stiff drink! Trees and crystals are capable of transmuting our excess energy, and rather than assume they'll 'eat' your heavy energy, *ask* and most of the time you'll get a "yes" along with the idea that this will make fertilizer or extra nutrition for the flora and fauna all around them. Nature also appreciates being thanked, and that gratitude sets up an increased interest in your well-being. You are taking care of you, emptying your cart from time to time, and nature is able to sense when you are ready to receive more of what you tend to celebrate with her.

Society 'at large' (pun intended) encourages addictions; "You must reward yourself with a treat," when you've achieved a goal. This is a pattern worth ditching because achievement is its own reward. You can, instead, call in your guides and celebrate in a more spiritual way, for lasting satisfaction.

If, by Rudyard Kipling

If you can keep your head when all about you
Are losing theirs and blaming it on you;
If you can trust yourself when all men doubt you,
But make allowance for their doubting too:
If you can wait and not be tired by waiting,
Or, being lied about, don't deal in lies,
Or being hated don't give way to hating,
And yet don't look too good, nor talk too wise;

If you can dream - and not make dreams your master;
If you can think - and not make thoughts your aim,
If you can meet with Triumph and Disaster
And treat those two impostors just the same:
If you can bear to hear the truth you've spoken
Twisted by knaves to make a trap for fools,
Or watch the things you gave your life to, broken,
And stoop and build 'em up with worn-out tools;

If you can make one heap of all your winnings
And risk it on one turn of pitch-and-toss,
And lose, and start again at your beginnings,
And never breathe a word about your loss:
If you can force your heart and nerve and sinew
To serve your turn long after they are gone,
And so hold on when there is nothing in you
Except the Will which says to them: "Hold on!"

If you can talk with crowds and keep your virtue,
Or walk with Kings - nor lose the common touch,
If neither foes nor loving friends can hurt you,
If all men count with you, but none too much:
If you can fill the unforgiving minute
With sixty seconds' worth of distance run,
Yours is the Earth and everything that's in it,
And - which is more - you'll be a Man, my son!

Chapter 31

LIVING JEWELLERY

My elemental Spiritual guides showed me via a lucid dream how gemstones which were once living creatures, and termed biogenic, reach out to heal people who are otherwise not open to holistic anything. This dream featured Lisa, who I knew to be anaemic and weak. Lisa walked into my dream dressed like an English duchess, very pale with her platinum blonde tresses piled up in a loose bun. She was wearing a pale pink satin evening dress with a white fur bodice. Lisa looked gorgeous, for the time period when it was fashionable to be feeble, and her dress was lovely, yet the combined effect looked ghostly. She was holding a light pink coral necklace and that's where I stepped in as a healer's assistant to the coral which suggested I swap Lisa's necklace for my orange and grey one. Lisa accepted the suggestion and seconds after I'd fastened the clasp her circulatory system started to flow with renewed vigour while, simultaneously, the grey in the coral highlighted the steel blue of her now vibrant eyes. I'd sensed that richer coloured coral would speed up the flow and supply of nourishment to her Lisa's blood cells, and saw proof of this happening.

In the same dream I was prompted to wear pearls, while writing, because they are skilled at bringing out truth, sincerity and intrinsic intelligence. They also contribute their own 'two cents worth' and were fashionable in the Second World War, when women were required to excel in a variety of roles.

Amber, solidified resin from pine trees and often containing insects, is also used in a holistic way. Children wear it round their necks to relieve pain when teething and adults wear amber pendants to attract or revitalise a love match. Amber, itself a time capsule, is popular with travellers.

Ammolite has been recently discovered in the Canadian Rockies. Once a living creature, it is now a multicoloured gemstone, which brings more oxygen into our lungs (an antidote to cancerous cells.) Ammolite is also a teacher/ facilitator of abundance; especially when worn close to our hearts.

My friend Amy Newsom has a fondness for biogenic gemstones and she specialises in making jewellery from ammolite.

You can reach her at **www.amynewsomdesign.ca**.

Chapter 32

GARDENING

When I walk into a garden which is teeming with life, full of beautiful vegetables all seeming to be smiling, I feel I am in a holy place. I know that I am in the company of the elemental kingdom and am not surprised when a butterfly dances in front of my eyes as if to say, "Hello Beautiful come and join the party." I could be naked and no-one would see me because I'd be sheltered by a huge Swiss chard leaf as I reached for tomato candy from a stem that thinks it is a giant beanstalk.

I celebrate gardeners. I love walking amongst and eating the fresh produce. I would find it a great challenge to have to manage without organic, newly picked fruit and vegetables. And I am grateful.

If you have a green thumb, then this is an aspect of Speaking Universal. The food you grow has so much more taste and nutrition than the produce which may begin its life in a farm but is then packaged, labelled, stored and then shipped across an ocean. Eating the foods in season where we live makes a lot of sense. By doing this we don't need to rely on supplements because we're getting the goodness directly from our food.

I wouldn't consider myself a gardener, yet I do have knack with roses. They are my favourite flower and wherever I've lived, they've bloomed all year for me. It wasn't 'til I discovered St Theresa, also known as 'Little Flower,' had a gift for getting roses to blossom in all weathers, that I knew this was a special thing. I am delighted that Great Spirit talks to me through my favourite flower, and also pretty happy to have Theresa as a middle name.

You may enjoy the following story about one of my roses Speaking Universal.

While I was living in Kelowna, my friend Edna's husband died, so one day I went to cheer her up, taking with me a single white rose representing enduring love. Edna thanked me, we chatted and she gave the rose pride of place in the centre of her dining table. About a month later, she emailed me a photo of the rose growing roots, and in that photo we both could clearly see the image of Jim's face. She had proof Jim was waiting for her, continuing to send love daily, and I had a visual reminder that Spirit works miracles.

Chapter 33

CHRIST CONSCIOUSNESS

This is a channelled chapter. I've asked Archangel Gabriel to be my muse.

The whole point of my coming to Earth was to show my family and friends that things are not as they seem; to live the legacy left by all ascended masters and demonstrate we can be in two places at once. We can have a coffee break with an angel or a poet from the past, and then switch our focus to an everyday task such as peeling potatoes with mindfulness.

Christ Consciousness is a frequency of vibration. Thirty three attempts to describe this from a numerological perspective. This frequency is light, pure, compassionate, joyful and agenda-free. It is pure unconditional love.

When witnessing the miracle of childbirth or a peaceful death we also experience joy, peace and awe. Our hearts swing wide open and emotion leaks from our eyes because we are part of a Heaven on Earth moment.

You can attain Christ Consciousness by allowing yourself to be entrained, by keeping company which elevates you and turning on your heel when you sense the conversation is likely to be banal and discouraging. Christ Consciousness is neither rooted in religion nor is it reserved specifically for human beings. Jesus is famous for having embodied Christ Consciousness.

He has been quoted as saying, "You shall do all these things and greater and, if you have the faith of a mustard seed, you can move mountains."

Many masters, some here on Earth, embody Christ Consciousness. They are ready to entrain and encourage us to put our innate talents to practical use right now on Earth. Facing difficulties is considered par for the course, because if we don't experiment we won't know the extent of our genius.

All 'we' have to do, you and me, is remain heart-centered, ditch any beliefs in fate, swap duality for infinite possibilities, and take bold action *for* Peace on Earth. When we focus on this, instead of expecting 'them' to do something for us, we harness the super-natural and very powerful effects of pure love energy and usher in *this* New Age of Enlightenment.

Does this idea call you? I have faith that it does.

Everyday Examples of Speaking Universal

- Tune in prior to making a phone call or answering the phone.
- Choose a greeting which will contribute to someone's day because "Hi, how are you?" has become impersonal, and people sense this.
- Offer practical assistance when you notice a piece of equipment is dangerous.
- Pay attention to telepathic, beamed messages, from your plants and pets.

- Respect a person's or pet's need for space when they are obviously not in the mood to chat or be stroked.
- Go inside prior to making a decision, and do the ABC technique. It only takes a couple of minutes and can be done unobtrusively.
- Prior to signing a contract, get a sample, preferably three samples, of the other party's handwriting with signature. I still do handwriting analysis, and you may contact me for an overview. Truth likes to reveal itself.
- Tell the truth, and be transparent. If you were not in the office one day when a client dropped by, just say so, no need to elaborate or apologise.
- Buy wholesome, fresh food from health food stores and farmers' markets. Shop locally and support your community including local businesses whenever you can.
- Take care of your car; it is more than a machine. Our energy influences the mechanical and electrical systems around us.
- Limit your exposure to radiation/electro-magnetic fields.
- Walk to the store. Stop and smell the roses on the way.
- Be polite to your employer and don't get drawn into drama-type gossip.
- Take the time to engage your children in meaningful conversation.

ABOUT THE AUTHOR

Victoria Fabling is a prolific writer of inspirational books and in Speaking Universal she gives you a proverbial press pass so that you can make life-changing connections and enter into successful joint ventures with masters, seen and unseen. You will find that "when two or more are gathered in *my* name" means two living beings, connected with Source, co-create miracles.

Victoria communicates on subtle levels with living beings, and invites you to give this a go. The results will add richness to your already awakened life. Victoria feels most at home with creative individuals and the elemental kingdom. Victoria is currently living on Vancouver Island working as a shaman (teacher) who facilitates healing transformations for people, pets and places.

Feel free to contact her via **www.myspiritualmentor.com** of via Fun with Fables – Victoria Fabling on Facebook

Printed in the United States
By Bookmasters